SWIMMING BETWEEN ISLANDS

Charlotte Eichler was born in Hertfordshire and studied English Literature and Russian at the University of Nottingham. She has an MA in Norse and Viking Studies, also from Nottingham. Her debut pamphlet, *Their Lunar Language*, was published by Valley Press in 2018 and a selection of her work was featured in Carcanet's *New Poetries VIII* in 2021. She lives near Leeds.

SWIMMING BETWEEN ISLANDS

CHARLOTTE EICHLER

CARCANET POETRY

First published in Great Britain in 2023 by
Carcanet
Alliance House, 30 Cross Street
Manchester, M2 7AQ
www.carcanet.co.uk

A CIP catalogue record for this book is
available from the British Library.

ISBN 978 1 80017 137 4

Book design by Andrew Latimer
Printed in Great Britain by SRP Ltd, Exeter, Devon

MIX
Paper from
responsible sources
FSC
www.fsc.org   FSC® C014540

The publisher acknowledges financial
assistance from Arts Council England.

Supported using public funding by
ARTS COUNCIL
ENGLAND

CONTENTS

Islomane	11
Divination	13
Baby Swimming	14
Clean White Bones	15
David	16
Bathroom Ghosts	17
At Mirror Lake	18
What Little Girls Are Made Of (i)	19
Goblincore	20
Backstage	21
The Rec	22
Brimstones	23
A Pheasant	24
A Meditation of Small Frogs	25
Trapping Moths With My Father	26
Autumn at the Wireworks	28
The Fifty-Year Traffic Jam	29
1,000 Porcelain Eggs	30
Malham Tarn	31
Walking Dragline Excavator	32
Saltburn-by-the-Sea	34
What Little Girls Are Made Of (ii)	36
Balloonist	37
Mary, 1903	38
Woman and Wall	39
The Babies and the Dahlias	40
Emergency	41
Cephalophores	42
The Navigator	43
What Little Girls Are Made Of (iii)	44
Ant Farm	45

Survivors   46
At the Cathedral of the Spilled Blood   47
52 Sovetskaya Prospekt   49
The Coffin Calendars   51
Halfway to Voronezh   52
How To Do Nothing   53
What Little Girls Are Made Of (iv)   55
Hervör and Völund   56
Owlish   57
Valkyrie   58
Kaktovik   59
Into the Fjords   60
Fata Morgana   61
Siri's Island   62
Uninhabited   63
The Hermit of Treig   64
Pabbay Cliffs   66
Mousa, Shetland   67
Asteroidea   68
Swimming Between Islands   70
Note   71
Acknowledgements   72

For my family

SWIMMING BETWEEN ISLANDS

ISLOMANE

'Islomania – a rare but by no means unknown affliction of spirit.
There are people [...] who find islands somehow irresistible. These
born "islomanes" [...] are direct descendants of the Atlanteans.'
– Lawrence Durrell, *Reflections on a Marine Venus* (1953)

She thinks of unhatched things:
eider weaving slippery nests
from the surf,

sharp rains
of skua and tern
when she strays from the path.

Some days she misses people
and sees them in seals
strung out in lines beyond the breaking waves.

With a toe in the water,
she leaves rows of pleated shells –
wedding dresses

and the trees filling
with a robin's twisted
ribbons of song.

✢

DIVINATION

We knew everything, playing oracle on the carpet.
Saturdays crawled with our ladybird circus –
from the ends of our fingers, solemn as blood,
          we sent them to find our future husbands.
We let them trickle down
          our wrists into the birdbath
to see if they'd keep walking while we drowned them,
jealous of their easy flight

          from one shape to the next.
Now, like hanged men, we want to buy futures
and there's someone doing tarot at the end of Brighton Pier.
          Stars are poking holes in the sky.
              There's an airy clatter

          of cards falling into place
but stranger things are happening beneath our feet:
coppers chink through the boards
          onto rows of starlings
stacking themselves like decks, noisy as a masked ball.
          We think *fluke* has something to do with wings
then remember whales, gliding
              despite the weight of all they know.
We watch the stragglers find their place under the pier,
          all the sea's dark spread ahead of us.

BABY SWIMMING

My friend and I each take a twin
      into the pool – when we dip them
they come up laughing,
      lashes spiked like urchins.

I am not their mother,
      I don't know the words to these songs.
Surprising how hard it is
      to hold the slippery egg
of his belly as he kicks and kicks

      propelling us round this aquarium.
We're breathing bleachy steam
      with strangers passing by and glancing in.
Am I holding him wrong?

      I am that fish with a see-through head
and all its machinery on show –
      tubes pulsing, bulbous green eyes
scanning up to the light –
      we hardly know what all the parts are for.

CLEAN WHITE BONES

Two cuttlefish are waving
in their glassy world
as I go to hold your hand.
Our fingers clash –

is it any easier
for them, with twenty
legs to tangle,
six hearts to please?

They speak a patterned language
of moody stripes and flashes,
the signs of love imprinted
on their skin

then leave their eggs
like a dropped necklace –
ruffled inklings of themselves
suspended in each blackened bead.

I shift and break our grasp,
thinking of the jewel you offered,
of all their hearts
and our half-hearted kisses.

If we could take their place
there'd be no mess,
just our children in the weeds
brightening like bulbs.

DAVID

Six foot five and all you eat:
a single bowl of mackerel
and a one-inch square of bread
to 'toast the Queen'.

       Coming from a bath,
your body's brittle coral,
your spine
       a seahorse curve.

I wish I could see

       your blue heart
through the pane
       of your skin

because you never
       answer questions,

flicking light
       from yourself

          like a shoal.

BATHROOM GHOSTS

I'm trapped in the en suite,
throwing shells from the window –
oysters, limpets, a mermaid's purse.

Their seaweed bodies, heads like drains.

I clean instead of breaking down the door,
dragging a man o' war from the plughole,
trying to read the hair on tiles.

Little sprite, licking grime off bathtubs.

Each mirror is a rockpool
full of unexpected mouths
and almost-children.

Girls, armies of girl ghosts,
third floor, third stall along.
Haunted backpacks and bruised hips
from throwing themselves at doors.

Some fishing nets are hard to see,
big enough to hold cathedrals.

A river child will join you –
it is roughly humanoid and loves cucumber.
Its head is a bowl of water you must keep full.

AT MIRROR LAKE

It took us by surprise, how fast the moon rose –
a stone thrown from the cliff

floating loose in hot blue sky.
We asked why, as if its grey bloom

in the day was extraordinary.
Our words clipped, unkind with fatigue.

I watched your profile – the suddenly unfamiliar
curve of your nose. We thought we knew

how things like day and night
and love would work.

I held you too hard, my nails
made chilly little moons along your arm.

WHAT LITTLE GIRLS ARE MADE OF (I)

She peels shells from flowerpots,
waits till they unfurl
and presses each cool body
to her skin. Her mother calls –
she leaves with snails
suckered to her legs like kisses.

GOBLINCORE

We knew we weren't right
under our clothes – our tiny wings,
our fur. We practiced eye contact
on frogspawn at the bottom of the garden.
There were hens and eggs lying
under bushes in their shamble nests –
the bubbled panes of glaire
between our fingers, the yolk
a golden toad on your palm!

We've grown to like our faces wild,
our chin spikes, our cobby goblin bodies.
We love grass stains, the taste of green
as you split a blade and owl it.
We live life close to the ground
crouched and smoky,
sharing each other's illnesses,
taking them on like charms.

Egg's broken morning, egg's freckled skin –
it's always summer with the warm bodies
of our hens and sisters.
On winter days your tongue's
an ice lolly in my mouth.
We wake with hair like frozen twigs
and kick through the windows of puddles.

BACKSTAGE

We fidget and wait for our cues.
Long John Silver, ten years old,
back broad and manly in his woollen coat

and me, three years below, transfixed.
He carries my parrot on his shoulder.
His name – Tom –

gives off an emerald light.
I touch his coat, not knowing
why, and wish I could sing

like the big girls, that I could tuck
my bottom lip the way they do.
A space in my brain has opened:

one day it'll fill with – who knows
what? Front gardens and cars?
Hosepipes? Something

to do with a bed? Right now
it's the sound of a wooden leg
thumping on stage

and I'm at the edge of a painted cliff,
the sun chucking handfuls
of tinselly stars on the sea.

THE REC

We lie on the roundabout staring
at the playground sky. Our feet slither
lazily along the tarmac, clouds spin
like slow clockwork.
We're eating *Lion* bars and sherbet,
mouths full of sequins.

There's a low hum around us,
static clicks round the edge of a field.
New kinks bloom at random:
cartoon foxes, Barbies,
a man's voice on a cassette.
The way our teacher slams down books.

We phone an information hotline and learn something
about cucumbers. We invent a new language –
words we know stand in for ones we don't:
mice! pillows! fireworks!
New knowledge piles up –
cow parsley isn't named after Coward's Lane,
the arm shop's just missing an
F.

We're windows wiped of steam,
dandelions blown clean and spiky.
We take long walks through buttercups,
stick our fingers in their foamy collars,
get licked by a cow's white tongue.

BRIMSTONES

sulphuric, angular days

the river's choking on white flowers
a slow, living ache
in her belly

each step
kindles yellow butterflies
from hedges

A PHEASANT

Beside us, copper tail cocked –
Aladdin's lamp.

A MEDITATION OF SMALL FROGS

i.

look –

climbing through moss

crisp seams
down their backs

ii.

curl your hand
under them gently

three cool bellies
on your palm

slimy intimacy
with earth

iii.

let them go

longtoeing back
to the stream

tiny gold rings
in their eyes

TRAPPING MOTHS WITH MY FATHER

You come to life as you name them:

swallow-tailed

        twenty-plumed

              spectacled

camouflaged by day, like you.

      Endlessly arriving on our beams of light

dust-soft

     drifts of them

          printing the white sheet.

Our heads lean close in this midnight silver

and our breath
     curls together in the cold.

Look closer:
         their dark wings are inscribed

            with eyes and feathers,

hieroglyphs you understand but can't explain.

They speak a lunar language

and wish they could go back.

AUTUMN AT THE WIREWORKS

It's spring again
but inside out,
the woods piratical,
bejewelled with pick-me reds,
gem-studded puffballs,
funnels of unlikely blue.
There are teaspoons
of jelly, dead men's fingers,
brains that glow.

Here we are unburied –
we lug our spirits
and our winter fears
in backpacks until we find
the waterfalls and whisky pools,
the woods' distillery
with copper guts
and leaf clot underfoot.

THE FIFTY-YEAR TRAFFIC JAM

sits tyre deep in sphagnum moss
surrounded by cracked glass
and rusting fern.

In spring, blue tits
hurl themselves at wing mirrors
and oily pools collect

electric dragonflies
with copper wire wings.
The forest

drinks them in,
sucks up radiator fluid
and cogs –

its creaking branches
sound, by the day,
more metallic.

1,000 PORCELAIN EGGS

Eggshell blues and greens,
brown speckles flicked
from our brushes.
Crackle glazes
close enough to fool
a cuckoo finch.

They lay on tins of cotton wool,
eggs of ortolan and oriole,
a toe-level cloudscape.

It's like painting faces
from memory, from broken mirrors.

On opening night, we
tap on the shells
using our nails as eggteeth.

MALHAM TARN

A skylark rises through fog,
the sun whirring in its throat.

WALKING DRAGLINE EXCAVATOR

Oddball, a rare beast,
gentle horse-head,
inches up the slope

on giant feet. The Aire's
flowing backwards,
upending itself in the ground,

opening a map
of broken hulls and pottery.
The old ways,

hats, tobacco, malt,
when the sky was a river of smoke.
This is the place

of the sunshine miners,
the day bats, owls
on the hillside at noon.

Oddball stops
on wooden pallets
with moths who come out

in bright weather.
Kestrels nest
in her cables,

reedbeds fill with the sound
of blown bottles, edges
creep with snipe.

There,
the gap-toothed power station
in a wild carrot sky.

SALTBURN-BY-THE-SEA

Parents stand in spaced-out
        queues for ice cream.
A man wears a t-shirt saying NORMAL.

There are no shells, no gulls,
a single seal off the end of the pier. NO DIVING.

A boy in a long black robe glides
        up and down the beach
collecting oily feathers.

The dogs are all so happy
and so jealous of each other.

Away from the crowd
        the sand is starred with upturned
crabs, legs flaring
in the pools left behind by the tide.

A vinegar wind begins –

the water's warmest at the edges
        where seaweed hangs;
my feet grow cool, green skin.

Up on the cliffs, chalk signs warn
YOU ARE LOVED.

It's all the colour of stones,
        brighter than you think –

the land is falling into the sea,
sprouting never-before-seen flowers.

WHAT LITTLE GIRLS ARE MADE OF (II)

Sharing out the money spiders,
circling them around her head for luck.

Sellotaping extra leaves
to three-leaf clovers.

BALLOONIST

Haworth Gala, 1906

She is wet to the waist
in river, a minnow girl
slipping through lanes,
always looking
for the ropes

somebody hangs
in the woods
near water,
or that feeling you get
at the edge of cliffs.

On the moors
the walls lose
their footing,
lurching up hills,
along scars.

She looks down on the village,
pictures it wilder –
black hats a penguin circus,
the Old White Lion
roaring her name –

all those extra hearts
to bloody her.
She chooses
the balloon's silky bones,
a lampfish sky.

MARY, 1903

I call it dollhousing. I start small,
wrapping things in newsprint –
hairpins, cotton reels, ribbons –

the tiny things we're taught to care about –
mustard tins and milk cans
piling up in the corner of the glasshouse.

We're high above the terraces,
mothers, grandmothers inside,
backs so sore they move like wooden dolls.

Father calls me *poison bottle*. Daughter –
that plodding word full of unspoken things.
Not like son – brief and blazing.

I take a match. The grass is full of speedwell,
blue eyes watching. The butterflies all closed,
ashy underwings like burnt letters.

Oh, to be at the centre of things –
a thumbnail frog on a lily pad,
the drop of blood on Queen Anne's Lace,

the spreading ripples that show
where a stone was
before it disappeared.

WOMAN AND WALL

After Mohammed Issiakhem's 'Femme et Mur' (oil on canvas, 1978)

Unasked, a question mark
bends the walls
of my body,

small hands press
the bars of my ribs.
Blue filters

through us – it is almost day
or nearly night. These walls
are the town's violet limits

bristling with storks.
I used to be glad
I wasn't a boy, no need to fight

or decide what to be.
Now I have two hearts, new hands
leached from bone

leaving me toothless,
cheeks pigeon-grey.
This wall is covered in

names – it should be easy
to choose one.
Hunched in half light

the storks clack beaks
with their chicks, a hard
kind of love in dirty nests.

THE BABIES AND THE DAHLIAS

There are babies under our chairs, around our feet. We pick them up
and put them on the table; they sit flower-faced and angry.
When my boss and I aren't looking, they amble to the map room

to paint our new world map. They use fingers to draw countries
that we've never found. I secretly admire them, despite my boss.
He tells me to organise my filing and use more yellow post-its

so I'm planning on the kitchen wall in pen. It leaves a greenish cloud
above the light switch. The babies are covered in wet paint,
writing slogans we will never understand. Outside, beyond the hedge,

are purple dahlias I want to pick: my boss says I can if we hurry
but when we get there it's the Village Show, trestle tables covered
in white food. We can't see the dahlias.

EMERGENCY

A line of white, unmarked cars
turns down our street.
Each contains a human
form, wrapped in cloth.

Sweet grubs,
swaddled, peaceful –
we can't tell
if they're leaving,
arriving, getting born
or dying. It's all the same

to us. Our house
has no doors
or window panes
but it's warm and full
of light –
straw on the floor,
a fire in the grate.

We rearrange our cupboards,
tend the snowy creak of freezers.
The sirens are always
in our ears – they sound
like ice cream vans
in minor keys.

CEPHALOPHORES

My favourite type of saint
is carrying his head.
He's not too attached to it,
offers it to anyone who asks.
Take his head from him

and his body wanders happily
through gardens, feeling
the colours of flowers,
the grass between his toes.

He can't speak
but the ivy is covered in commas –
if he stands still long enough
they settle on him
like the gaps between clouds.

Meanwhile, his head is all mine –
someone to talk to on the bedside table.
Someone to tell me to buy bleach
and birthday gifts.

A second head, though,
can make you unsure of your own.
I give his back and he takes it

gratefully, preparing, always,
to swap his head for sky
and pass it on.

THE NAVIGATOR

Your hands don't look like yours,
the skin dough-pale and grazed.
I think of how we used to walk on walls
holding onto those huge thumbs,
even the narrow black railings by the river,
one foot in front of the other

faster and faster.
You were so used to fear –
swallowing it quick like scalding tea
in the mess, battling fog
over the world shrunk to a map –
we thought it was invisible to you,

although later you remember
where the graze came from:
walking home with us you'd dragged
your hand along the wall until it bled
to keep you conscious
so we wouldn't be afraid.

WHAT LITTLE GIRLS ARE MADE OF (III)

A green itch:
she pinches little wings
then plucks a leg.
A glass bead grows in its place,
the way some weeds she picks
confess white sap.
More cluster round a rose:
she is making lines of limbless flies.
Ants leave a trickle of red
down her thigh.

ANT FARM

i.

anatomical slice
through the heart
of a house

legs waving
egg-busy dark

huge porcelain babies
carried aloft
awkward as furniture

ii.

ropes above our heads link the nest
to a tank of plants – the ants march to
and fro along them holding green banners

iii.

we are islands off
the antway, don't
deviate, don't fall
into the water, don't

forget the burning
kiss of family
the formic scent
of home

SURVIVORS

Aunts drink tea for hours – they have no mirrors or clocks
but each other's faces tell the time.

Why do their hands shake and rattle the cups in their saucers?
We prowl the flat – the hallway dark with years of coats,

the dining room with carpets on the walls.
Each visit we think something will be different

but there's always the same red View-Master
with unchanging views of Prague, and no TV.

We draw elaborate tunnels and hold funerals for bees;
the cheese plant grows towards the window.

Our aunts show us a glass case of curled-up figures.
All we want is the china cockatoo and toy koalas.

Their arms come towards us lined with numbers –
we wriggle away from their touch.

AT THE CATHEDRAL OF THE SPILLED BLOOD

We buy eggs   painted with the silence of snow
scarves wrapped tight   around our mouths
Ice crystals prickle our noses   when we breathe

Mum's hiding the vodka from granny   in a high cupboard
She arrives in a red fur coat   a basket of freshly baked buns
the smell of nutmeg and cabbage

The men have eyes red from drink   as they tell us again
the story of the sack   the car boot   the journey south
They stand at the edge of the room   like grandfather clocks

Baby sister is in her cot   wise old face turned
from a single piece of birch   We carry her inside us
sisters   mothers   grandmothers

wrapped in coats and scarves   until we're round as matryoshka dolls
lined up at the market   beside the painted eggs
Our steps grow louder   the farther we are from home

the darker it gets among the trees
When a car pulls up to the kerb   my boots bite the ice
like a clenched jaw   the glass winds down with a hiss

Devushki   he's saying   *Sing for us!*
Of course you can sing   pretty girls like you
and I'm not sure if it's him   or granny speaking now

We're weaponised and vitreous   ponytails brittle with frost
Under our coats   our hip bones slice our lilac jeans
The men are out of the car   blocking the pavement

Granny's hanging the eggs   in the window
Their glitter's more real   than the street outside
the red dots might be us   in the snow

52 SOVETSKAYA PROSPEKT

I'm haunted by the story of a sack.
My coat smells of the unneutered male cat
who is not allowed outdoors.
I have local boots, the high heels help me
to blend in and are useful on the ice.
Cabbage sizzles blackly in the kitchen,
where flies fly in perfect squares
around the light. It's minus 11,
pancakes are steaming the window.

The story of the sack comes from another country.
Another country and I'm the one
who's changed. Even my handwriting's new –
the m's have lost their scaffolding and curled up
in my mouth. I'm forced to act in a play
in a language I don't speak
and I like it.

Who told me the story of the sack?
Two men have moved into the apartment,
they can't find their country on the map.
Our building is always being redecorated.
The neighbours come downstairs
to have sex in our kitchen,
escaping husbands who are never there.

But back to the story of the sack.
I argue with the men over who is more of a visitor.
Our arguments are long and involved
because they don't speak English
and neither do I. They wear frilly aprons
in the daytime and make sure I get enough to eat.

At night they get drunk and tell me about a girl they knew
who was put in a sack and forced to get married.
Her family wouldn't take her back and I hate myself
for thinking, maybe she was happy? Choice removed,
kitchen, children, watermelons all summer.

I take my coat from underneath the cat.
The feathered girls in bright balaclavas –
their knees bend backwards like birds' legs!
I join them. We skitter
on snow.

THE COFFIN CALENDARS

Miss June is given lilies, Miss
December's in white fur. In the woods,
twelve walnut caskets for us to stand
in. Childhood Sundays, the moth-eyed
rows of old men, half-living. *Memento
mori* paintings hanging on the walls,
the angels in the aisles with noseless
shadows. My smile says too much
about my skull. I try to stay still – the
photographer says next year we'll all
have guns and camouflage bikinis. In
town, people turn their heads as far as
owls do. Our dresses show the winged
blades of our backs as we fly off the
shelves – and the men, the men joke
they   can't   see   the   coffins.

HALFWAY TO VORONEZH

On a stopped train,
sharing the chocolates
your fiancée gave you
for the journey,
trying not to giggle
as two men gut fish
on the table below,
the carriage filled
with blood and sea.
The stations we pass
look temporary,
concrete platforms
without signs.
An unreal place
that doesn't count.
When the heating breaks,
it only makes sense
to share warmth.
The train pulls into the city
and before you leave
we get coffee,
watching twelve brides
round a statue, posing
in varying shades of white.

HOW TO DO NOTHING

The train has stopped
among grasses.
There's a crash
each time it tries to move –
someone thinks we're hitting deer.
Kiti and I have nothing

to say to each other;
George is doing pull-ups
in the doorway.
The food car's empty
and the icons on my phone
have turned folkloric:

owls, hares, decorated
skulls in earthen tones.
I try texting
but the messages
are muffled,
cable-knit words.

The trackside's an embroidery
of flowers – meadowsweet
and foxtail, vetch and toadflax.
Chestnut hoverflies
and double-bees.
Someone sends glasses of tea

down the carriage.
We still our hands
on the warmth.
We're starting to talk –
the umms and ahhs
spread like weeds.

Instead of news,
we speak of driving cars
on frozen lakes,
picking blueberries in swamps.
Kitchen dentistry.
The woman who walks her pig.

WHAT LITTLE GIRLS ARE MADE OF (IV)

The sun buzzes
in its jar of sky.
She runs, bee-striped,
arms out like wings.

HERVÖR AND VÖLUND

I held the birds of myself together
for seven years.
When I left with his ring,
he made seven hundred

to tempt me back.
Offered earrings like green eyes,
brooches of milk teeth,
silver cups like small skulls.

I put our sky-blue eggs
beyond his reach,
up where distance
softened everything to feathers.

I loved his hands,
their blacksmith skill.
He loved black velvet bark
after a fire.

But it wasn't only metal he could shape.
Now he's far above me,
a vulture with black fingers
and a blood-drop head.

Our children's veins were green-lit –
young trees
with the smell of smoke
already in their branches.

OWLISH

Promised an owl, we wait hours
picking over the indigestible
parts of our day –
needle-fine bones,
soft fur dropped at our feet.

I'm nested in your jacket's down,
winged by your arms,
half in the place where trees
smoke into cloud.

VALKYRIE

Swans settle down to sleep among the cabbages,
        wings touching like the paper dolls
                she strings across her door.

She watches from the window,
        thinks of all the words she knows for dark.
                Tonight, she goes to them –

they croak to each other, their bright beaks,
        the bow curves of their necks.

                She looks back to her house
                        and her arms feather in the cold.

KAKTOVIK

We hear it singing songs of solid ice

Our children dance in dirty sandals

                on the slick black head of a whale,

the islands by our town   all eyes.

We share out red insides,
            braise sourdock and blubber,
press round the warmth of cigarettes.

            Winter comes anyway –

the snow sprouts claws,

            pads through the streets after dark,

cracks its teeth on the bones we left behind.

By the icehouse a mother
            licks new colours from her fur,

far from her blue world

            and the cub that melted as they swam.

Our homes are barred with shovels, antlered –
            she's close enough to taste the glass.

At night, wind flutes through the whalebones –

INTO THE FJORDS

Someone's turned over
                    a mirror, the grey-backed sea
                    a polished image of the sky.

Waterfalls pour upwards,
                    meeting themselves at the shore –
windows in pieces on the water,
                    sills waving –

whole villages submerged and shimmering.

Clouds hide a wreck,
                  a ship's broken ribs, splintered

like this edge of land – leaning over
the bow, I see myself
capsized.

FATA MORGANA

Water has caught this place –

      rivers split and trap houses
so they're swimming   next to barnacled cars
      as cod leap up to line roofs.

Salt crusts everything – the grass crackles with it.

Kittiwakes nest on the windowsills
      painted red to match their tongues
and girls' hair is brown and shiny as seaweed –

      their boats hover
just above the harbour –

everything made of unreachable light.

SIRI'S ISLAND

She has arched, pixelated eyebrows
　　　　that arrived bobbing in a box
　　　　　　　　on the North Atlantic.

Her face is rainproof,
　　　　she wakes
　　　　　　　beneath a net of geese,

　　　　　　　　lapwings bleeping.

The light is a mix of night and day,
　　　　moss-green glow.

　　　　The island's heart,
　　　　　　　scrolling waterfalls:

Last windmill in Iceland?
World's smallest post office?
How do eiders work?

Boats pass
　　　　full of house plants, rugs, video games.

　　　　　　　Soggy cardboard and sea gooseberries hang

in the water
　　　as the world delivers itself
　　　　　　to her harbour.

She speaks all our languages.

　　　　Her stories end at *Once upon a time.*

UNINHABITED

The grass that pours down the cliff
is dotted with beaks –
even the rocks are alive
and whistling, hiding red legs.
The shoreline blinks

as each piece of kelp is turned
and, where the land shatters
into the sea, plankton hang
like blown glass,
invisible without their sparks.

THE HERMIT OF TREIG

Eagles tilt the hills,
the loch's skin bends
like a fish. This isn't solid

ground – even the train tracks float
on brushwood. My legs give way

from time to time.
How nice to have an accident!
Knocked back into my body
for a spell, careful bandages.

I built a house from matchsticks
then from trees. Shed full
of cowberries drying
on the year's old news.

I live in a cloud world, one day
behind. Snow falls,

small things get lost.
The rose I was talking to
last night has gone –
I'll find her,

chop the wood
before the ice

comes back. It's pretty,
what I'm seeing –

zigzags every colour
you can think of.

PABBAY CLIFFS

Belly to grass,
greenish jelly sea
below. Here,
next to my face,
miniature worlds of moss:

tiny trees and stars,
near and far
as the queue of strangers
behind me
waiting their turn

to look down
at the guillemots
hidden by the cliff's
pleats, each precariously
at home.

O warm egg bodies,
the rocks look soft
enough down there,
greened with weed.

In the distance
killer whales,
fins tall as you.

MOUSA, SHETLAND

Airy flies cloud round our feet
from rotting seaweed, black
with a salt wrack smell.

Petrels flit from a Pictish broch
as we climb the steps at dawn.
We are found:

the gannets are white flares
hitting the water
under a fishbone sky.

ASTEROIDEA

The sea is far above
my head like the sky
in a child's drawing.
Instead of stars, starfish:
brittle, spiny, bloody henry,
crown-of-thorns.
Blue-deep fish,
pyjama sharks,
a shoal of swans
with silver feet.
There's a lone
diver in red
drifting like kelp.
How will he get down?
My abalone toenails
scrunch the sand.
Strange that I can hear
so much. Should coral
squeak like clean hair
as it grows? Do fish
jangle like cutlery?
This might be the sea
after all – a place
among currents where sharks
in black and grey stripes
swim past too fast to notice.
It's raining jellyfish.
They fall at my feet
like things in jars.

SWIMMING BETWEEN ISLANDS

The island you were born on
is crammed with cabinets
and grandfather clocks.

Nearby, the island of children
with its shrieks and red tapestries
and the island of *one day, when.*

You have the sea and its bed,
a silvery current of hair
and a necklace of eggs

where a hundred new things grow.
The horizon looks toothed
but those are more islands:

the island of slow translation,
the island of choirs. An island of frogs
who spend their lives inside flowers.

On some you'll find you breathe better
underwater than in their thundery air.
Soon you'll have an island forest,

ribcage ferns exhaling green.
Swimmers will come to your house
to borrow your eyes.

NOTE

'Walking Dragline Excavator'

'Oddball' is the nickname of the Bucyrus Erie BE 1150 dragline excavator machine at RSPB St Aidan's nature park. The land at Swillington, near Leeds, was an opencast coal mine until it was flooded in 1988 when the riverbank collapsed.

ACKNOWLEDGEMENTS

Many thanks to the editors of the following journals and anthologies in which some of these poems first appeared: *Agenda, Anthropocene, Blackbox Manifold, The Flambard Poetry Prize 2015, The Interpreter's House, The Island Review, The Manchester Review, New Poetries VIII, PN Review, The Rialto, The Scotsman, Stand* and *Strix.*

'Woman and Wall' won the English-language category of the Barjeel Poetry Prize in 2020 and 'Kaktovik' was commended in the Battered Moons poetry competition in 2016.

I am very grateful to *Poetry London* for awarding me a place on their 2017/2018 mentorship programme with Anthony Vahni Capildeo, whose guidance, wisdom and reading recommendations were invaluable.

Thank you to everyone who has helped with the poems in this book, especially the University of Leeds poetry group – John Whale, Jason Allen-Paisant, Anthony Vahni Capildeo, Ian Fairley, Rachel Bower, Malika Booker, Carole Bromley, Lydia Kennaway and Mick Gidley. Thank you to Emma Storr, Antony Dunn, Nashwa Nasreldin, Jen Campbell, Suzannah V. Evans and Penny Boxall for your feedback and encouragement over the years. Particular thanks to John McAuliffe and Michael Schmidt for your editorial insight and support.

Most of all, love and thanks to Ricky, Bill, Cansu, Mark, Marie and my parents.